1 MONTH OF
FREE
READING

at

www.ForgottenBooks.com

By purchasing this book you are eligible for one month membership to ForgottenBooks.com, giving you unlimited access to our entire collection of over 1,000,000 titles via our web site and mobile apps.

To claim your free month visit:

www.forgottenbooks.com/free912210

ISBN 978-0-265-93524-8
PIBN 10912210

This book is a reproduction of an important historical work. Forgotten Books uses state-of-the-art technology to digitally reconstruct the work, preserving the original format whilst repairing imperfections present in the aged copy. In rare cases, an imperfection in the original, such as a blemish or missing page, may be replicated in our edition. We do, however, repair the vast majority of imperfections successfully; any imperfections that remain are intentionally left to preserve the state of such historical works.

March 25, 1939   Number 343

THE UNIVERSITY OF NORTH CAROLINA RECORD

THE GRADUATE SCHOOL

DIVISION OF PUBLIC HEALTH

CATALOGUE ISSUE
1938-1939

Announcements for the Session
1939-1940

THE UNIVERSITY OF NORTH CAROLINA PRESS
ISSUED 12 TIMES A YEAR AS FOLLOWS: 4 NUMBERS IN FEBRUARY, 3 NUMBERS
IN MARCH, 3 NUMBERS IN APRIL, 1 NUMBER EACH IN JUNE AND OCTOBER
ENTERED AS SECOND-CLASS MATTER AT THE POSTOFFICE AT
CHAPEL HILL, N. C.
UNDER THE ACT OF AUGUST 24, 1912

CATALOGUE OF EVENTS

SESSION 1939-1940

1939

June 4-6	*Sunday through Tuesday.* Commencement Exercises.
Sept. 14	*Thursday.* Registration for the fall quarter.
Sept. 15	*Friday.* Class work for the fall quarter begins.
Oct. 6	*Friday.* General Meeting of Graduate Students and Faculty, 8 p.m., Smith Building.
Oct. 12	*Thursday.* University Day.
Nov. 29	*Wednesday.* Thanksgiving Recess begins (1:00 p.m.).
Dec. 4	*Monday.* Thanksgiving Recess ends (8:30 a.m.).
Dec. 8-16	*Friday through Saturday (1:00 p.m.) of following week.* Registration for the winter quarter.
Dec. 12-16	*Tuesday through Saturday (1:00 p.m.).* Examinations for the fall quarter.
Dec. 16 (afternoon) Jan. 1, 1940	Christmas Recess.

1940

Jan. 2	*Tuesday.* Registration of new students.
Jan. 3	*Wednesday.* Class work for the winter quarter begins.
Mar. 8-16	*Friday through Saturday (1:00 p.m.) of following week.* Registration for the spring quarter.
Mar. 12-16	*Tuesday through Saturday (1:00 p.m.).* Examinations for the winter quarter.
Mar. 17-24	*Sunday through Sunday.* Spring Recess.
Mar. 25	*Monday.* Registration of new students.
Mar. 26	*Tuesday.* Class work for the spring quarter begins.
June 3-7	*Monday through Friday.* Examinations for the spring quarter.
June 9-11	*Sunday through Tuesday.* Commencement Exercises.

OFFICERS OF ADMINISTRATION

FRANK PORTER GRAHAM, M.A., LL.D., D.C.L., D.Litt., *President*
ROBERT BURTON HOUSE, A.M., *Dean of Administration*
WILLIAM WHATLEY PIERSON, Ph.D., *Dean of the Graduate School*
WILLIAM DEBERNIERE MACNIDER, M.D., Sc.D., LL.D., *Dean of the School of Medicine*
CARL V. REYNOLDS, M.D., *State Health Officer, North Carolina State Board of Health*
MARK V. ZIEGLER, A.B., M.D., *Senior Surgeon, U. S. Public Health Service; Regional Consultant, Interstate Sanitary District No. 2, U. S. Public Health Service*
MILTON JOSEPH ROSENAU, A.M., M.D., *Director*

ADMINISTRATIVE COMMITTEE

WILLIAM WHATLEY PIERSON, Ph.D., *Dean of the Graduate School*
WILLIAM DEBERNIERE MACNIDER, M.D., Sc.D., LL.D., *Dean of the School of Medicine*
HERMAN GLENN BAITY, A.B., S.B. in C.E., S.M., Sc.D., *Professor of Sanitary Engineering*
EDWARD MACK, JR., Ph.D., *Smith Professor of Chemistry*
JOHN BROOKS WOOSLEY, Ph.D., *Professor of Economics*
HAROLD WILLIAM BROWN, A.B., M.S., Sc.D., M.D., Dr.P.H., *Professor of Public Health*
MILTON JOSEPH ROSENAU, A.M., M.D., *Director*

FACULTY

MILTON JOSEPH ROSENAU, A.M., M.D., *Professor of Epidemiology*
HERMAN GLENN BAITY, A.B., S.B. in C.E., S.M., Sc.D., *Professor of Sanitary Engineering*
DANIEL ALLAN MACPHERSON, Sc.M., Ph.D., *Professor of Bacteriology*
HAROLD WILLIAM BROWN, A.B., M.S., Sc.D., M.D., Dr.P.H., *Professor of Public Health*
JAMES CLARENCE ANDREWS, B.S., Ph.D., *Professor of Biological Chemistry-Nutrition*
JOHN WILLIAM ROY NORTON, A.B., M.D., M.P.H., *Professor of Public Health Administration*
.., Professor of Venereal Diseases
MICHAEL ARENDELL HILL, JR., A.M., *Associate Professor of Mathematics*
HAROLD BENEDICT GOTAAS, B.S. in C.E., M.S. in C.E., S.M. in San. Eng'g., *Assistant Professor of Sanitary Science*
CARL V. REYNOLDS, M.D., *Associate Professor of Public Health*
ALBERT JOHN SHELDON, B.A., M.A., Sc.D., *Instructor in Public Health*
THOMAS J. BROOKS, JR., B.S., M.S., *Assistant in Public Health*

*To be appointed.

LECTURERS (1938-1939)

MARK V. ZIEGLER, A.B., M.D., *Senior Surgeon, U. S. Public Health Service*

JOHN H. HAMILTON, B.S., M.D., *Director of State Laboratory of Hygiene, N. C. State Board of Health*

WARREN H. BOOKER, C.E., *Director, Division of Sanitary Engineering, State Board of Health*

GEORGE M. COOPER, M.D., *Director, Division of Preventive Medicine, N. C. State Board of Health*

ERNEST A. BRANCH, D.D.S., *Director, Division of Oral Hygiene, N. C. State Board of Health*

LESLIE C. FRANK, B.S., C.E., *Senior Sanitary Engineer, Sanitation Section, U. S. Public Health Service*

LOUIS L. WILLIAMS, JR., M.D., *Senior Surgeon, Malaria Investigations, U. S. Public Health Service*

JESSE H. EPPERSON, B.S., F.A.P.H.A., *Superintendent of Health, Durham City-County Health Department, Durham, N. C.*

WILLIAM ANDERSON OLSEN, A.B., A.M., *Associate Professor of English, The University of North Carolina*

JOSEPH C. KNOX, M.D., M.P.H., *Director, Division of Epidemiology, N. C. State Board of Health*

ROBERT E. FOX, A.M., M.D., M.P.H., *Director, Division of County Health Work, N. C. State Board of Health*

ROBERT T. STIMPSON, A.B., M.D., C.P.H., *Director of Bureau of Vital Statistics, N. C. State Board of Health*

WILLIAM P. RICHARDSON, A.B., M.D., C.P.H., *District Health Officer and Instructor in Public Health for Social Workers*

WILLIAM MAURICE COPPRIDGE, M.D., *Chief of Urological Staff, Watts Hospital, Durham, N. C., Venereal Diseases*

WALTER REECE BERRYHILL, A.B., M.D., *University Physician and Associate Professor of Medicine, The University of North Carolina*

JANE D. GAVIN, R.N., B.S., *Supervising Nurse, Orange-Person-Chatham District Health Department and Supervisor Rural Training for Public Health Nursing Students*

HERMAN F. EASOM, M.D., *Director, Division of Industrial Hygiene, N. C. State Board of Health*

L. M. FISHER, D.P.H., *District Engineer, Interstate Sanitary District No. 2, U. S. Public Health Service*

GEORGE M. LEIBY, A.B., M.D., M.P.H., Dr.P.H., *Consultant, Venereal Disease Control, N. C. State Board of Health*

JAMES A. WESTBROOK, B.S. in C.E., M.S.E., *Chief Sanitary Engineer, Orange-Person- Chatham District Health Department*

GENERAL INFORMATION

Chapel Hill is located thirty miles west of Raleigh, the Capital of the State, and the headquarters of the State Board of Health. The University of North Carolina is in the beautiful Piedmont section of hills and forests and entered from every direction by paved roads. It is near the center of the State, midway between the mountains and the sea. There is convenient bus service several times each day from Greensboro, Raleigh, and Durham. It is in an environment of natural beauty and simple culture, age, and traditions.

In 1936 a Division of Public Health was established and a Director appointed. The University of North Carolina, at Chapel Hill, has been designated by the United States Public Health Service as the center for the training of health officers for the Interstate Sanitary District No. 2, extending from Delaware to Florida, to carry out the provisions of the Social Security Act for the training of public health personnel.

The Division of Public Health enjoys the active cooperation of the State Department of Health at Raleigh. Members of the staff give exercises in their special fields and the students have the opportunity to see the practice and study the methods and material of an efficient State Health organization at first hand.

Cooperation is also maintained with Duke University and its Hospital, as well as with Watts Hospital, in Durham. Furthermore, we enjoy the cooperation of the local health officer at Durham, who, through lectures and practical demonstrations, gives the student an opportunity to see the health work of a city government, where, as well as at Raleigh, opportunity is offered for special study and investigation of health problems.

For county health work a Field Demonstration Unit has been established in the Orange-Person-Chatham District Health Unit for the purpose of giving trainees practical experience in rural health administration.

Students are enrolled in the University of North Carolina and enjoy all the rights and privileges of the general student body. They may take courses in other departments of the University, provided they are properly qualified and have the approval of the Administrative Committee. Certain courses in economics, political science, sociology, social work, and statistics are regarded as having an especially close relationship to public health.

The administration reserves the right to refuse admission to any student who is, in its judgment, not qualified to profit by work in the Graduate School, to limit the number of students admitted to any course, and to drop from the roll any student whose work it deems unsatisfactory for any reason. All applicants for admission will be assumed to have assented to these conditions.

The Division of Public Health is geographically and spiritually in the School of Medicine, with which it maintains close cooperation. Academically, it clears through the Graduate School and those interested are advised to consult the Graduate School Catalogue.

Graduate degrees offered by the Division of Public Health are administered by the Graduate School of the University of North Carolina. These degrees are: Master of Public Health (M.P.H.), Doctor of Public Health (Dr.P.H.), Master of Science (with designation) (M.S.), Doctor of Philosophy (with designation) (Ph.D.).

All requirements concerning these degrees are administered by an Administrative Committee of the Graduate Division of Public Health with the approval of the Administrative Board of the Graduate School.

The Certificate in Public Health (C.P.H.) is not considered a graduate degree and is, therefore, administered by the faculty of the Division of Public Health in the School of Medicine.

PURPOSE AND PROGRAM

The object of the Division is to provide the scientific ground work which underlies sound public health administration. To this is added some acquaintance with modern public health procedures of a selective type. The program includes lectures, sanitary surveys in the field, various exercises and laboratory work by members of the faculty, supplemented by special instructors actively engaged in public health problems. Students may select the courses in their curriculum to prepare themselves for careers in teaching, administration, field or laboratory positions. Special opportunity is offered to those who desire to contribute knowledge through laboratory research or field investigations.

To this end programs of study are provided, but special programs to meet aptitudes and to fit in with prior training and experience may be arranged.

Each graduate student works under the direction of the Administrative Committee of the Graduate Division of Public Health established for this purpose by the Graduate School. The program and plan of study proposed by each graduate student must be approved by the above Administrative Committee.

The effort is made to arouse in the mind of the student a feeling that graduate work is not a matter solely of attendance on classes and passing examinations in courses. He must see his work as a whole and in its relation to a department of learning, not as a set of isolated units. In the more intimate personal relations to the Administrative Committee, too, he finds values impossible in the undergraduate course. He is a member of a small group; instruction is more nearly personal; he becomes acquainted with the method as well as the content of learning.

The *Doctor* of Public Health degree and the Ph.D. (with designation) are therefore not granted as a result of accumulating credits in courses, but depend upon scholarship as revealed in class and laboratory work and seminars and examinations, and also as demonstrated in a dissertation based upon scientific investigations showing thoroughness to which is added an indication of scientific imagination.

Development of precision and method in investigation and the cultivation of powers of criticism and evaluation of evidence, together with the enlarged mastery of the subject matter of a defined field, constitute a training of indisputable value to the students who plan to enter the profession of public health. Research is the way of progress in each of its activities.

It is recommended that students who enter any phase of public health work should have adequate courses in physics, chemistry, and biology, and in the basic medical sciences, structure of the body and its functions both normal and abnormal. For advanced study a knowledge of French or German is important.

GRADES

Grades for those taking graduate courses are as follows:

Passed: which represents satisfactory work.

Failed: which represents work unsatisfactory for graduate credit.

No work falling below the standard represented by the grade *Passed* is counted for graduate credit. No grade, on a mathematical basis, below 80 will be credited. If, in the judgment of the Administrative Committee, the quality of the work done by any student falls below the standard expected of graduate students, the registration of such a student will be canceled.

Work done *in absentia* will not be counted for graduate credit, except that in certain cases approved by the Division and by the Administrative Committee, part of the work on the thesis for a higher degree may be done elsewhere. All such work, even when credited, is subject to examinations at the finals required for the degree.

MEDICAL ATTENTION

In order to provide proper attention for the student during sickness, the University employs four full-time physicians and maintains a well appointed infirmary. The infirmary is equipped with all necessary conveniences and comforts, and with a modern X-ray unit and laboratory for diagnostic purposes under the direction of a full-time technician. It is under the immediate supervision of the University Physician and is provided with four experienced nurses. At the discretion of the University Physician a student may be admitted to its wards, and for such services as may be rendered by the staff no charges are made. But, should any additional service (consultation, special nurses, operations requiring the attendance of a trained surgeon) recommended by the attending physician and approved by the parent or guardian, be necessary, the student will be required to pay for such services.

RECREATION

The University gymnasium and five large athletic fields provide ample facilities for exercise and recreation, all under the supervision and direction of a well-organized Department of Physical Education.

LIBRARIES

In addition to the specialized departmental and school libraries, the general University library, containing more than 360,000 volumes, offers its opportunities to members of all divisions of the institution. Current periodicals are available in the reading room of the Division of Public Health. The Library of the School of Medicine is available, being in the same building. The Library of the School of Medicine at Duke University—ten miles from our campus—is open for use of our students.

TUITION AND FEES

The tuition is $83.34 a quarter. In addition the following University charges for each quarter are:

*Matriculation	$20.00
Student publications	2.30
Student Union Fee	1.00
Student Entertainment Fee	1.00
	$26.30

A laundry deposit of $8.50 is required a quarter. Any balance not used is refunded to the student at the end of the quarter.

FELLOWSHIPS AND SCHOLARSHIPS

Graduate scholarships and fellowships are available under the jurisdiction of the Division of Public Health. Application for these should be made to the Director.

Fellowships and scholarships for trainees under the Social Security Act are available to properly qualified candidates. Application for these should be made to the State Health Officer of the State in which the applicant has residence.

MICROSCOPES

Each student is requested to bring a microscope.

---

*This fee includes fee for physical education, the library fee, the fee for infirmary service, the fee for registration costs, the fee for debates (.17), and membership fee in the Athletic Association ($3.33).

DORMITORY ACCOMMODATIONS

Subject to prior reservation, dormitory accommodations are available in the University dormitories, room rent ranging from $68.50 to $90.00 for the nine months, or $34.50 for the fall quarter, price depending upon the location of the room. This includes light, heat, and service. All rooms in the dormitories are completely furnished. Students will, however, provide their pillows, bed linen (for single beds), blankets, and towels. The University is building a new dormitory within one block of the new medical building, designed primarily for medical and graduate students, which will be ready for occupancy in September, 1939.

Requests for dormitory reservations should be addressed to The Cashier, The University of North Carolina, Chapel Hill, N. C. A deposit of $6.00 is required.

It is important that students confer with the Secretary in the office of the Division of Public Health before making arrangements for living accommodations in the village.

BOARD

The University Dining Hall Cafeteria is under expert management. Food of excellent quality and variety is served at cost.

Board without room can be obtained in the village from $22.50 to $35.00 a month.

REGISTRATION

Registration is subject to the regulations of the Graduate School.

REQUIREMENTS FOR DEGREES

MASTER OF PUBLIC HEALTH

Admission: Students matriculating for this degree must be graduates of approved medical schools. Before admission to candidacy for the degree of Master of Public Health, the student will be required to present an acceptable program of advanced study covering one year's work, including a major subject of study and fundamental courses in at least some of the following: public health administration, epidemiology, sanitary engineering, statistics, and bacteriology.

For the degree of Master of Public Health one academic year must be spent in residence at this University. The final examination is both written and oral and based upon the program of study outlined by the student and accepted by the Administrative Committee of the Graduate Division of Public Health. Only students whose records in the various courses indicate a high type of scholarship will be admitted to this examination.

The work outlined above can be done in one year by students whose preparation has been good and by those who devote themselves with application to this special work.

DOCTOR OF PUBLIC HEALTH

This degree is not given as the result of accumulation of credits in courses but depends upon scholarship as revealed in class and laboratory work and seminars and examinations, and especially as demonstrated in a dissertation based upon scientific investigations showing thoroughness to which is added an indication of scientific imagination.

The Doctor of Public Health degree is regarded as a professional graduate degree in that it is limited to those who have a medical degree.

The requirements for the degree are not measured in terms of time but quality of work. A well prepared student of good ability may secure the degree upon the completion of two years of graduate study following the medical degree. It should, however, be understood that this time requirement is wholly secondary to other considerations. In some instances work done in other institutions may be counted toward the degree, at the discretion of the Administrative Committee of the Graduate Division of Public Health. Under no circumstances will the degree be awarded until the student has been in residence at least three consecutive quarters within a period of twelve months.

REQUIREMENTS

1) Those having a medical degree from a recognized school will be accepted provided they satisfy the Administrative Committee that they are qualified.

   Those who have a M.P.H., or its equivalent, from a recognized institution of learning will be admitted provided they satisfy the Administrative Committee that they are equipped for intellectual advancement with investigative capacity.

2) *A Preliminary Examination:* A qualifying examination which is intended to search the depth and breadth of the candidate's learning and mentality, as well as to reveal his promise of productive scholarship. The preliminary examination is oral and may include a knowledge of the natural and physical sciences and languages; if deficiencies are disclosed, a candidate may be advised or required to take courses to make up such deficiencies.

3) *Scientific Investigation:* Research which must be individual, but under supervision. The data collected by personal investigation shall be used as the basis of the dissertation.

4) *A Dissertation:* A dissertation which shall be a scholarly study of the subject investigated with a survey of the literature, discussions, and conclusions.

5) *Final Examination:* A final examination based upon the dissertation and the subjects of the candidate's field.

DOCTOR OF PHILOSOPHY IN PUBLIC HEALTH

The degree of Doctor of Philosophy in Public Health is conferred only upon those who have completed, with high distinction, a period of extended study and investigation in a single field of learning, during which they have gained control of the materials in the chosen field, have mastered the method of advanced study, and have illustrated this method through a dissertation, the result of independent research, which adds to the sum of human knowledge or presents results that have enduring value. Neither the accumulation of facts, however great in amount, nor the completion of advanced courses, however numerous, can be substituted for this power of independent investigation and the proofs of its possession. While a well prepared student of good ability may secure the degree upon the completion of three year's study, it should be understood that this time requirement is wholly secondary to other considerations.

The requirements for the degree, as they pertain to admission, transfer of credit, admission to candidacy, residence, course of study, grades, foreign languages, dissertation, examinations, etc., are the same as those prevailing generally in the Graduate School. Students should consult the Catalogue of the Graduate School for detailed information in this connection. For the preliminary information of persons who contemplate becoming candidates for the degree, the following summary of requirements is given:

Admission: A bachelor's degree from a recognized institution.

Residence: A minimum of three years of graduate study, at least one of which must be at the University of North Carolina.

Languages: The student is required to have a reading knowledge of two modern foreign languages, one of which must be either French or German.

Admission to Candidacy: Application for admission to candidacy for the degree must be filed one academic year, or three quarters, in advance of the date at which the degree is expected.

Program of Study: The student will take major courses covering adequately the field of major interest and at least six courses in a minor, which may or may not be in a different field. Not more than three courses, or fifteen hours a week of class attendance, will be permitted in any one quarter.

Examinations: (a) A preliminary oral examination, not earlier than the end of the second year of study, and at least one academic year prior to commencement at which the degree is expected.

(b) A written examination in the field of major interest given at least four weeks before the end of the period of study.

(c) An oral examination covering the entire field of study given at least one week before the time at which the candidate expects to receive the degree.

Dissertation: The subject of the dissertation shall have been approved at the time of the preliminary oral examination and must be presented in final form at least six weeks before the time at which the candidate expects his degree.

MASTER OF SCIENCE IN SANITARY ENGINEERING

The curricula leading to this degree are designed to prepare for careers in the engineering divisions of national, state, and local health agencies; in municipal public works and service organizations; in such industries as involve sanitary problems; and in professional engineering organizations' engaged in the investigation, design, supervision of construction, and operation of sanitary works.

Admission: Candidates for this degree are better equipped for their work if they hold an engineering degree from an institution of recognized standing, preferably in civil, chemical, or mechanical engineering, where the curriculum has involved fundamental work in chemistry, physics, mathematics, and the engineering sciences. However, holders of a baccalaureate degree from a college of approved standing may be admitted to candidacy provided they demonstrate an aptitude for the natural sciences and have taken fundamental courses with high credit in chemistry, mathematics, physics, and the engineering or biological sciences.

Residence: Ordinarily two academic years must be spent in residence at the University of North Carolina. Students who have graduated with high credit from approved engineering schools, and who do not desire a considerable number of courses in public health subjects closely related to sanitary engineering, may be able to satisfy within one year the minimum requirements for the degree, which are specified below. However, it is strongly advised that students take the two-year curriculum in order to be able to include such important related subjects as epidemiology, communicable diseases, public health administration, bacteriology, parasitology, malariology, vital statistics, economics, report writing, public speaking, and public administration, in addition to their courses in engineering and sanitary science. Furthermore the two year course provides more time for the satisfaction of the language requirement, the conduct of an investigation, the formulation of the thesis, and preparation for the comprehensive examinations.

Language Requirement: A reading knowledge of one modern foreign language is required. This knowledge will be tested by a special examination given by the language department concerned, and must be certified to before the student is admitted to candidacy for the degree.

Admission to Candidacy: Application for admission to candidacy for the degree must be filed six months, or two quarters, before the date at which the degree is expected. Admission is based upon the satisfaction of requirements recited in detail in the catalogue of the Graduate School.

Program of Study: Considerable latitude is allowed the student in the selection of courses to build a curriculum best suited to the particular field of public health engineering in which he expects to engage. At the time of his admission the student will be required to present an acceptable program of study covering his period of residence. This program must include a minimum of nine courses (45 quarter hours) of graduate grade, at least six of which shall be in the field of major interest and at least three in an allied minor field. All courses which are to be counted for graduate credit must be passed with a grade, on a mathematical basis, of at least 80. Not more than three courses of fifteen hours of class attendance will be permitted during each of the quarters of the final year of study.

Examinations: Candidates for this degree are required to pass all examinations in courses at the end of each quarter of residence. Courses offered for graduate credit shall be passed with the minimum grade specified above. In addition, two special examinations are required: (a) a written examination covering the field of major interest shall be taken not earlier than the first month of the last quarter of residence; and (b) an oral examination, covering the entire work of the candidate, both major and minor, with a period of time especially reserved for the defense of the thesis, which shall be given at least one week before the time at which the candidate expects to receive the degree.

Thesis: The candidate is required to present a thesis at least one month before the time at which the degree is expected to be conferred. This thesis is designed to test the candidate's knowledge of the method of investigation and his ability to make use of the knowledge he has acquired. Its subject must be connected with the major and related to a course or courses pursued in residence. It must show independent thought both in its recognition of a clearly defined problem and in its method of treatment. Major credit, not to exceed one course, may be given for the thesis.

Graduate School Regulations: The candidate is referred to the catalogue of the Graduate School for detailed regulations and requirements relating to this degree, which are, in general, the same as those pertaining to the Master of Arts and Master of Science degrees.

MASTER OF SCIENCE IN PUBLIC HEALTH

The curricula leading to this degree are intended to prepare students for careers in various divisions of public health activity, and the degree itself is to be interpreted as semi-professional in character. Courses of study are offered which are designed to prepare for pursuits in the following fields:

1. Public health engineering
2. General sanitation
3. Public health statistics
4. Supervision of sanitary works

Admission: Candidates for this degree are usually better equipped for their program if their preliminary training has included a substantial amount of work in the physical, chemical, and biological sciences. Holders of a baccalaureate or engineering degree from an approved institution may be admitted to candidacy for the degree, provided their prior work has been of a satisfactory order and has included courses in such sciences as are basic to the field of study in which they propose to engage.

Residence: At least one academic year must be spent in residence at the University of North Carolina.

Language Requirement: No foreign language requirement is imposed.

Admission to Candidacy: Application for admission to candidacy for the degree must be filed six months, or two quarters, in advance of the date at which the degree is expected.

Program of Study: In the selection of courses the student is allowed considerable latitude. However, his program must be formulated at the time of his admission, and approved by the Administrative Committee of the Graduate Division of Public Health. Although the general regulation of the Graduate School regarding majors and minors does not apply in this case, the program must be balanced, integrated, and designed to fit the student for a definite field of activity. The course load is not limited by quarters, but it should be moderate and balanced. The program must include at least nine courses (45 quarter hours) of work bearing graduate credit, which must be successfully passed.

Examinations: Candidates for this degree are required to pass all examinations in courses at the end of each quarter of residence. Courses carrying graduate credit must be passed with a grade, on a mathematical basis, of at least 80. In addition, a written examination covering the field of the student's principal interest must be taken not earlier than the first month of the last quarter of residence, and an oral examination covering the entire work of the candidate, shall be taken at least one week before the time at which the candidate expects to receive the degree.

Thesis: No thesis is required for this degree.

Substitute Award: Students who are candidates for this degree who fail to comply with all of the requirements therefor, but who satisfy the requirements for the Certificate in Public Health, may receive this latter award.

THE CERTIFICATE IN PUBLIC HEALTH

The certificate in public health (C.P.H.) is not an academic "degree" and is therefore administered by the faculty of the Division of Public Health in the School of Medicine. The certificate in public health (C.P.H.) is intended to train students to carry on one of the varied phases of work in the field of public health. A basic program is offered to comprise the important sanitary sciences underlying sound public health administration. The curriculum is elastic to provide for prior training, individual aptitudes, and special interests. It may be either diversified or concentrated in a special field.

The certificate in public health is based upon satisfactory completion of an approved curriculum or for meritorious work in a special field. The basic program of study should include courses in public health administration, epidemiology, sanitation, vital statistics, and public health laboratory.

At least one academic year must be spent in residence in the Division of Public Health at the University of North Carolina.

The requirements for admission are met by the following:

a) Graduates of approved medical or engineering schools.

b) Graduates with a bachelor's degree from approved colleges, including a substantial amount of satisfactory work in the premedical, physical, and social sciences. Before starting courses in public health students should first obtain credits in the basic medical sciences, viz:- anatomy, physiology, bacteriology, pathology, etc., which may be secured at this University. Ordinarily it will take at least two years following the bachelor's degree to satisfy the requirements for the Certificate in Public Health (C.P.H.).

Special Students: Those who do not meet the academic requirements for admission may be accepted as special students provided they present evidence of training and experience which will fit them to benefit by the course given.

Special students may be granted the certificate if they complete an approved curriculum, achieve the honor roll with an average grade of "B" or better, and satisfy all other requirements. Otherwise, they will be entitled to a letter of attendance stating their grades.

SHORT COURSE

A short course is offered in the fall quarter to meet the emergency under Title VI of the Social Security Act. The short course is integrated with the fall quarter for the certificate in public health and is designed to give the student a general view of the present day scientific aspects of sound public health administration. The curriculum comprises laboratory courses, lectures, field demonstrations, and other exercises. After twelve weeks of intramural instruction, the student has the opportunity of taking one month of practical field work in the Orange-Person-Chatham District Health Unit, or in a similar unit in his own State in the Interstate Sanitary District No. 2.

REQUIREMENTS FOR ADMISSION

Each student is required to file a statement concerning his educational history and degrees, including an official transcript of college credits.

I. For Public Health workers with medical degrees:
   A medical degree from a recognized medical school. It is advantageous to have some experience in public health work.

II. For Public Health workers without medical degrees:
   a. For sanitary engineers a degree in engineering from an accepted university or technical school.
   b. For sanitarians, a bachelor's degree from a recognized institution of learning, including credits in at least two of the following sciences: chemistry, physics, biology.
   c. For sanitary officers, credits of college grade in at least two of the following sciences: chemistry, physics, biology.

III. SPECIAL STUDENTS. Practical experience may be accepted by the University in lieu of college courses, each case to be arranged with the Director.

Academic Awards: Those who comply with the entrance requirements under I and II above and who receive an average grade of C or better in an approved curriculum will be entitled to a document which states the completion of an approved course of studies, specifies the time of attendance, and designates whether the curriculum was designed to prepare for the work of health officer, sanitary engineer, sanitarian, or sanitary engineer.

Special students may be granted the above if they complete an approved curriculum, achieve the honor roll with an average grade of "B" or better, and satisfy all other requirements. Otherwise, they are entitled to a letter of attendance stating their grades.

Grades for the short course are based upon the following system of grading:

> Grade A, Excellent
> Grade B, Good
> Grade C, Fair
> Grade D, Barely passed
> Grade E, Conditioned
> Grade F, Failed
> Grade I, Incomplete work

The grade I may be converted into one of the other grades by completing within a period of twelve months such additional assignments as may be required by the instructor in the course. A grade of I not so converted becomes F.

SCHOLARSHIPS

Scholarships, including an allowance for expenses, have been allotted to the District of Columbia, Delaware, Maryland, Virginia, West Virginia, North Carolina, South Carolina, Georgia, Florida, and other States under the Social Security Act. Application for these scholarships should be made to the State Health Officer of the State in which the applicant resides or plans to work.

FEES AND EXPENSES—SHORT COURSE

The fees, including tuition, registration costs, infirmary service, and library fee, are $100.00 for the twelve weeks' period. All fees are payable in advance.

COURSES FOR GRADUATES AND ADVANCED UNDERGRADUATES

NOTE: Figures in parenthesis are those previously employed for similar or identical courses.

P.H. 111 (101). PUBLIC HEALTH ADMINISTRATION (3).

The theory of public health administration is developed by a study of the administrative methods actually employed in various governmental units including the federal government, states, municipalities, and counties. Certain phases of public health administration are covered by special lecturers who are invited from time to time to cover those particular fields upon which they can speak with authority.

Some time is given to proper procedures in the administrative control of the more important communicable diseases such as tuberculosis, venereal diseases, diphtheria, pneumonia, measles, whooping cough, meningitis, typhoid fever, intestinal parasites, rabies, and malaria.

Each physician taking the course is required to make a comprehensive public health survey of some assigned local health organization according to an outline supplied him, and supervised field trips are arranged for an afternoon each week.

Each student compiles his own text book during the course, using a loose leaf system. The notes on the lectures are supplemented by pamphlets, reprints, forms, and references to specific phases of the work, so that at the end of the course the student has the nucleus for a public health reference library which can be enlarged upon from year to year.

Three lecture hours a week, fall quarter. Professor Norton; special lecturers.

P.H. 113. CHILD HYGIENE (3).

A broad outline of the various problems relating to child health is presented: growth and development, nutrition, health appraisal, morbidity and mortality, maternal care, and the health protection of the infant, preschool, and school child. Visits are made to prenatal, infant and preschool, school, nutrition, mental hygiene, dental, and crippled children's clinics. Special emphasis is placed on the handling of problems in which preventive efforts of public health and cooperating agencies can be made particularly effective. *Three lecture hours a week, winter quarter.* Professor Norton; special lecturers.

P.H. 121 (141). VITAL STATISTICS (2).

The lectures outline methods of vital registration, the participation of local health departments in recording births and deaths, and the value of these records when properly used. Methods are presented for collecting, tabulating, adjusting, and drawing sound conclusions from statistical data regarding human life. Methods of graphic presentation of statistical data are studied, with special emphasis on their use by the county health officer and other members of the public health departmental staff. The calculations include population estimations, rates and ratios, and simple correlation. Laboratory work furnishes the student an opportunity to apply the principles covered by the lectures. *One lecture and two laboratory hours a week, fall quarter.* Professor Norton; special lecturers.

P.H. 122. MATHEMATICAL STATISTICS (5).

This is an advanced course in statistical methods (same as Mathematical Statistics 111) intended for those showing particular aptitude in Vital Statistics 121 and for those planning to specialize in the handling of statistical and observational data. The course deals with the elementary theory and applications of mathematical statistics to various medical and public health activities, treating in detail the following topics: graphs, averages, dispersion, skewness, sampling, probable error, frequency curves, and correlations. *Five hours a week, winter quarter.* Professor Hill.

P.H. 131 (122). COMMUNICABLE DISEASES (3). Prerequisite, General Zoology 41, 42 or Bacteriology 51.

Lectures, demonstrations, and practical laboratory work on the common communicable diseases. Emphasis is placed upon laboratory diagnosis, modes of transmission, and means of prevention. The laboratory work consists of the identification and study of the various organisms responsible for disease including filtrable viruses, rickettsia, bacteria, and spirochetes. For sanitary engineers, sanitarians, and sanitary officers. *Two lecture and two laboratory hours a week, fall quarter.* Professor Brown; Dr. Sheldon.

P.H. 151. PUBLIC HEALTH LABORATORY METHODS (4).

Lectures, discussions, and practical laboratory work in the diagnosis of diseases of public health importance, such as scarlet fever, diphtheria, tuberculosis, whooping cough, pneumonia, typhoid fever, bacillary and amoebic dysentery, brucellosis, gonorrhea, syphilis, rabies, malaria, and hookworm. Insect vectors are examined, and simple classification of mosquitoes attempted. The preparation, standardization, and use of biological products is discussed, and the student performs Shick, Dick, Widal, Wassermann, and Kahn tests. Emphasis is placed on proper taking of specimens, principles involved in diagnosis, and interpretation of results. *One lecture and six laboratory hours a week, spring quarter.* Professor MacPherson.

P.H. 161 (111). THE PRINCIPLES OF SANITATION (5).

A general survey course consisting of lectures, demonstrations, laboratory exercises, and field visits, designed to meet the needs of students preparing to engage in public health activities. The following subjects receive attention: historical and epidemiological background of sanitation; sanitary surveys; rural sanitation; water supply, purification, and distribution; sewerage, sewage treatment, and stream pollution; laboratory analysis of water, sewage, and industrial wastes; malaria control; illumination; plumbing; food sanitation; milk sanitation; shellfish sanitation; garbage and refuse collection and disposal; sanitation of schools, camps, and bathing places; heating, ventilation, and air conditioning. *Three lecture and four laboratory hours a week, fall quarter.* Professors Baity, Gotaas; visiting lecturers.

P.H. 162. SANITARY CHEMISTRY (5). Prerequisite, Chemistry 1, 2, 3, or equivalent.

A study of the principles of general, qualitative, and quantitative chemistry and their application to the procedures for the analysis for dissolved gases, organic and mineral content, and the physical properties of water, sewage, and industrial wastes, the origin of various chemical constituents and their interpretations. *Two lecture and six laboratory hours a week, fall quarter.* Professors Baity, Gotaas.

P.H. 163. SANITARY CHEMISTRY (5). Prerequisite, Chemistry 1, 2, 3, or equivalent.

Principles of quantitative analysis and biological chemistry and their relation to environmental sanitation; water and sewage bacteriology; chemical and biological investigations of water and sewage. *Two lecture and six laboratory hours a week, winter quarter.* Professors Baity, Gotaas.

P.H. 164. SANITARY CHEMISTRY (5). Prerequisite, P.H. 163 or equivalent.

The study of the principles of physical, colloidal, and biological chemistry and their application to problems in sanitary engineering. Experimental problems and investigations for the control and operation of sanitary works. Laboratory tests of plant reagents and special chemical tests of water and sewage. The student may devote part of the laboratory time to the investigation of a special problem in which he is interested. *Two lecture and six laboratory hours a week, spring quarter.* Professors Baity, Gotaas.

COURSES FOR GRADUATES

P.H. 201. EPIDEMIOLOGY (5).

A general course covering the more important facts on which scientific and sound public health administration is based.

PART I. Lectures and demonstrations covering the epidemiology of the important diseases, the laws of epidemics, principles of prevention, modes of infection, water-, milk-, and insect-borne diseases, seasonal prevalence, disinfection and quarantine, vaccination and immunity, illustrative epidemics and the management of an epidemic campaign. Each student makes a special study of the epidemiology of one disease which is summarized in a paper.

Practical field work in this course is done under the direction of the North Carolina State Board of Health in the Orange-Person-Chatham District and the Durham-City-County Health Departments. Immediate supervision of field work is under the guidance of the local health officers.

This is the first half of the course in Epidemiology which is concluded in Part II in the spring quarter. The course is divided in two parts without repetition.

Five hours of lectures, demonstrations, and seminars a week, fall quarter. Professor Rosenau.

P.H. 202. EPIDEMIOLOGY (5).

PART II. A continuation of Epidemiology 201.

Five hours of lectures, demonstrations, and seminars a week, spring quarter. Professor Rosenau.

P.H. 204. CLINICAL COMMUNICABLE DISEASE (3). Prerequisite, Degree in Medicine.

Lectures, demonstrations, ward rounds, and visits to patients with communicable diseases. The early diagnosis of communicable disease is stressed. Demonstrations are given of home isolation and nursing. *One lecture and three hours of ward work, winter quarter.**

P.H. 205. NUTRITION (3).

This course consists of a series of lectures dealing with the known dietary essentials, their chemical nature, distribution in nature, and the diseases resulting from their lack. Special emphasis is given to discussion of practical food sources of the various dietary essentials. Visits and ward rounds are made to hospitals and other institutions where clinical experience with deficiency disease may be obtained. *Three lecture hours and demonstrations a week, spring quarter.* Professor Andrews.

---

*To be arranged.

P.H. 206. EPIDEMIOLOGY—SYPHILIS (2½). Prerequisite, Degree in Medicine.

This course reviews the clinical, epidemiological aspects and control measures of syphilis. Practical work in diagnosis and treatment are secured in the clinics at Watts Hospital in Durham and the Orange-Person-Chatham District Health Department and the Durham City-County Health Department. *One lecture hour and three hours of clinic work a week, spring quarter.**

P.H. 211. PUBLIC HEALTH ADMINISTRATION (5).

This course is especially designed for the director of local health work. State and local public health problems of the Southeastern States are particularly stressed. Program planning, budget operation, relationships with cooperating official and non-official agencies, coordination of private and public health medical activities, health education, and similar problems which are handled by the health officer are studied. Weekly field trips are arranged to study the practical operation of different plans according to varying local needs. *Three lecture and four or more field trip hours a week, winter quarter.* Professor Norton; special lecturers.

P.H. 231. MEDICAL PARASITOLOGY (3). Prerequisite, Communicable Diseases 131 or General Zoology 41 and 42.

Lectures, demonstrations, field trips, and laboratory work upon the animal parasites of man. Special emphasis is placed upon the diagnosis of the presence of the parasites, their life cycles, and measures for control. Training is given in the identification of the various arthropod vectors of human disease. The laboratory diagnosis of malaria is stressed and consideration is given the biology and identification of the important mosquitoes of Southern United States. *Two lecture and three laboratory hours a week, spring quarter.* Professor Brown; Dr. Sheldon.

P.H. 232. PARASITOLOGICAL METHODS (5). Prerequisite, Medical Parasitology 231.

A consideration of the methods employed in parasitological study. Life cycles of the various animal and human parasites are carried out in experimental animals. The methods of preservation and mounting of parasites are studied and each student builds up his own collection. The techniques involved in the field studies of the various human parasites are considered. Mosquito surveys are made and special emphasis placed upon the identification and the biology of the *genus anopheles.* Each student builds up a personal reprint library in connection with the various problems studied. *Three lecture and six laboratory hours a week, spring quarter.* Professor Brown.

P.H. 233. MALARIOLOGY (5). Prerequisite, Communicable Diseases 131 or General Zoology 41 and 42.

Lectures, demonstrations, and laboratory devoted to the study of malaria in man and mosquito and methods of its control. The biology and classification of mosquitoes are considered, special attention being given to the species that transmit malaria. Each student participates in field work which includes a blood and spleen survey in a malarious area. Correlated with this is a mosquito survey of the same area. The specimens and data collected in the field are used for laboratory exercises. The control of malaria is discussed and field projects are visited. The student is instructed in the various engineering methods of mosquito eradication and control, and several laboratory periods are devoted to such subjects as mapping, surveying, drainage design, dusting, oiling, and screening. *Three lecture and four laboratory hours a week, spring quarter.* Professors Brown, Baity.

---

*To be arranged.

P.H. 261. MILK AND FOOD CONTROL (3). Prerequisite, P.H. 201, P.H. 131, P.H. 161.

Principles of milk and other food sanitation. Public health supervision and control of the production, processing, and distribution of milk and other foods. Lectures, field and laboratory work. *Two lecture and three laboratory hours a week, winter quarter.* Professor Baity; Dr. Kyker; visiting lecturers.

P.H. 262. LIMNOLOGY, RHEOLOGY, STREAM POLLUTION (5). Prerequisite, P.H. 162 and 163.

A study of the principles of limnology, rheology, and fresh water ecology, as they apply to water supply, sewage disposal, and insect control. Emphasis is placed on the physical, chemical, and biological factors of the aquatic environment, the identification and control of organisms common to reservoirs, stream pollution and self purification, the control of streams from the viewpoint of the public health and conservation, and the control of insects. *Three lecture and three laboratory hours a week, spring quarter.* Professor Baity.

P.H. 271. HYDROLOGY AND STATISTICS (4).

A study of meteorology, rainfall, stream flow, storage, and the statistical analysis of quantitative, hydrological, sanitary, and research data, making use of frequency curves, correlation, curve fitting, and nomograms. Theoretical statistics applied to physical measurements. *Four lecture hours a week, winter quarter.* Professor Gotaas.

P.H. 272. WATER SUPPLY AND SEWERAGE (5). Prerequisite, Hydraulics, Math., Strength of Materials, Math. 123.

The study of water consumption, sources of supply, drainage areas, and ground water development and control, storage and distribution oi water and their relation to the welfare of the community. The study of sewerage facilities, sewage flow, storm water drainage, and separate and combined sewers and their importance to the protection of the public health. *Three lecture and three laboratory hours a week, fall quarter.* Professor Gotaas.

P.H. 273. WATER PURIFICATION (4). Prerequisite, P.H. 272 and P.H. 162; corequisite, P.H. 163.

The theory and principles of aeration, coagulation, sedimentation, softening, deferrization, odor and taste removal, water plant management, and their application to the design and operation of water purification plants for the supply of a safe and potable water for municipal and rural communities. *Four lecture hours a week, winter quarter.* Professors Baity, Gotaas.

P.H. 274. SEWAGE TREATMENT AND WASTE DISPOSAL (5). Prerequisite, P.H. 273; corequisite, P.H. 164.

The nature and characteristics of sewage and industrial wastes which affect public health or create an undesirable public nuisance. A study of the principles of screening, grit removal, sedimentation, chemical precipitation, filtration aeration, disinfection, aerobic and anaerobic decomposition, sludge treatment and disposal, and their application to the design and operation of treatment facilities. The treatment and disposal of solid industrial and municipal refuse is also considered. *Three lecture and three laboratory hours a week, spring quarter.* Professors Baity, Gotaas.

P.H. 281. INDUSTRIAL HYGIENE AND SANITATION (5). Prerequisite, P.H. 162, P.H. 272.

A study of the relation of the industrial environment to the health, efficiency, and welfare of workers, including the following topics: industrial accidents, atmospheric impurities, occupational diseases, adverse temperatures and humidities, illumination, factory sanitation and inspection, and industrial legislation. The laboratory period will be devoted to the procedures used in the determination and interpretation of adverse working conditions, including physical properties of air and atmospheric impurities, and visits to factories. *Three lecture and three laboratory hours a week, spring quarter.* Professor Gotaas; other members of the staff.

RESEARCH COURSES

The courses described below may be continued for several quarters and for more than one academic year. Credit of 5 quarter hours or more may be earned each quarter in any course.

P.H. 301. ADVANCED EPIDEMIOLOGY.

A research course for those qualified to do independent investigation under supervision. Admission to this course only after consultation with the professor who must assign or approve the subject of research. A student may spend part or all of his time in research. *Ten or more laboratory hours a week.* Professor Rosenau.

P.H. 311. RESEARCH IN PUBLIC HEALTH ADMINISTRATION.

Individual arrangements may be made by the advanced student to spend part or all of his time in supervised investigation of selected problems in Public Health Administration. *Ten or more laboratory hours a week.* Professor Norton.

P.H. 313. RESEARCH IN CHILD HYGIENE.

The advanced student may undertake supervised investigation of special problems in school and preschool health or other phases of child hygiene activities. *Ten or more laboratory hours a week.* Professor Norton.

P.H. 331. RESEARCH IN PARASITOLOGY. Prerequisite, Parasitology 231.

Research problems may be undertaken by advanced students. *Ten or more laboratory hours a week.* Professor Brown.

P.H. 361. RESEARCH IN SANITARY SCIENCE. Prerequisite or corequisite, P.H. 201, P.H. 131, P.H. 161, P.H. 162, P.H. 163, P.H. 164.

Research problems in sanitary chemistry and biology, such as soil pollution, bathing places, industrial and domestic wastes, malaria control, milk and food sanitation, institutional and transportation sanitation. *Ten or more laboratory hours a week.* Professors Baity, Gotaas.

P.H. 371. RESEARCH IN SANITARY ENGINEERING. Prerequisite or corequisite, P.H. 162, P.H. 163, P.H. 164, P.H. 272, P.H. 273, P.H. 274.

Research in the engineering phases of problems relating to water supply purification, sewerage and sewage treatment, and stream pollution. *Ten or more laboratory hours a week.* Professors Baity, Gotaas.

P.H. 381. RESEARCH IN INDUSTRIAL SANITATION. Prerequisite or corequisite, P.H. 281.

Research in problems of industrial sanitation, such as the control of fumes, gas, dust, bacteria, and illumination. *Ten or more laboratory hours a week.* Professor Gotaas.

Lightning Source UK Ltd.
Milton Keynes UK
UKHW012329061118
331891UK00010B/1043/P